Defoe Abbott Marx Hardy Melville Montaigne Machiavelli Haggard Chesterton Cooper Emerson Joyce Austen Hugo Eliot Grimm

Stoker Carroll Christie Maupassant Byron Engels Molière Schiller Smith Kafka

Wilde Garnett Einstein Fitzgerald Hawthorne Dostoyevsky Willis Hall

Goethe Cotton Kipling Doyle

Baum Henry Nietzsche Balzac

Leslie Dumas Flaubert Turgenev Crane Verne

Stockton Vatsyayana Vinci

Burroughs Busch

Curtis Tocqueville Whitman Gogol

Homer Widger Tolstoy

Darwin Thoreau Twain Scott Harte

Potter Freud Zola Lawrence Plato

Kant Jowett Stevenson Dickens Hesse Burton

Andersen

London Descartes Voltaire Cervantes

Poe Aristotle Wells Cooke

Hale James Hastings Irving

Bunner Shakespeare Chambers

Richter Chekhov da Benedict Alcott

Doré Dante Shaw Pushkin

Swift Wodehouse Newton

Memoirs of Madame de Montespan —Volume 3

Françoise-Athénaïs de Rochechouart de Mortemart,
marquise de Montespan

Imprint

This book is part of TREDITION CLASSICS

Author: Françoise-Athénaïs de Rochechouart de Mortemart, marquise de Montespan
Cover design: Buchgut, Berlin – Germany

Publisher: tredition GmbH, Hamburg - Germany
ISBN: 978-3-8424-5337-1

www.tredition.com
www.tredition.de

MEMOIRS OF MADAME LA MARQUISE DE MONTESPAN

Written by Herself

Being the Historic Memoirs of the Court of Louis XIV.

BOOK 3.

CHAPTER XXXV.

M. de Lauzun and Mademoiselle de Montpensier. — Marriage of the One and
Passion of the Other. — The King Settles a Match. — A Secret Union. — The
King Sends M. de Lauzun to Pignerol. — The Life He Leads
There. — Mademoiselle's Liberality. — Strange Way of Acknowledging It.

They are forever talking about the coquetry of women; men also have their coquetry, but as they show less grace and finesse than we do, they do not get half as much attention.

The Marquis de Lauzun, having one day, noticed a certain kindly feeling for him in the glances of Mademoiselle, endeavoured to seem to her every day more fascinating and agreeable. The foolish Princess completely fell into the snare, and suddenly giving up her air of noble indifference, which till then had made her life happy, she fell madly in love with a schemer who despised and detested her.

Held back for some months by her pride, as also by the exigencies of etiquette, she only disclosed her sentimental passion by glances and a mutual exchange of signs of approval; but at last she was tired of self-restraint and martyrdom, and, detaining M. de Lauzun one day in a recess, she placed her written offer of marriage in his hand.

The cunning Marquis feigned astonishment, pretending humbly to renounce such honour, while increasing his wiles and fascinations; he even went so far as to shed tears, his most difficult feat of all.

Mademoiselle de Montpensier, older than he by twelve or four-teen years, never suspected that such a disparity of years was visible in her face. When one has been pretty, one imagines that one is still so, and will forever remain so. Plastered up and powdered, consumed by passion, and above all, blinded by vanity, she fancied that Nature had to obey princes, and that, to favour her, Time would stay his flight.

Though tired and bored with everything, Lauzun, the better to excite her passion, put on timid, languid airs, like those of some lad fresh from school. Quitting the embraces of some other woman, he played the lonely, pensive, melancholy bachelor, the man absorbed by this sweet, new mystery of love.

Having made mutual avowal of their passion, which was fill of esteem, Lauzun inquired, merely from motives of caution, as to the Princess's fortune; and she did not fail to tell him everything, even about her plate and jewels. Lauzun's love grew even more ardent now, for she had at least forty millions, not counting her palace.

He asked if, by the marriage, he would become a prince, and she replied that she, herself, had not sufficient power to do this; that she was most anxious to arrange this, if she could; but anyhow, that she could make him Duc de Montpensier, with a private uncontrolled income of five hundred thousand livres.

He asked if, on the family coat-of-arms, the husband's coronet was to figure, or the wife's; but, as she would not change her name, her arms, she decided, could remain as heretofore, — the crown, the fleur-de-lis, and so forth.

He inquired if the children of the marriage would rank as princes, and she said that she saw nothing to prevent this. He also asked if he would be raised higher in the peerage, and might look to being made a prince at last, and styled Highness as soon as the contract had been signed.

This caused some doubt and reflection. "The King, my cousin," said Mademoiselle, "is somewhat strict in matters of this sort. He seems to think that the royal family is a new arch-saint, at whom one may look only when prostrate in adoration; all contract therewith is absolutely forbidden. I begin to feel uneasy about this; yes, Lauzun, I have fears for our love and marriage."

"Are you, then, afraid?" asked Lauzun, quite crestfallen.

"I knew how to point the Bastille cannon at the troops of the King," she replied; "but he was very young then. No matter, I will go and see him; if he is my King, I am his cousin; if he has his crotchets, I have my love and my will. He can't do anything, my dear Lauzun; I love you as once he loved La Valliere, as to-day he loves Montespan; I am not afraid of him. As for the permission, I know our history by heart, and I will prove to him by a hundred examples that, from the time of Charlemagne up to the present time, widows and daughters of kings have married mere noblemen. These nobleman may have been most meritorious,—I only know them from history,—but not one of them was as worthy as you."

So saying, she asked for her fan, her gloves, and her horses, and attended by her grooms-in-waiting, she went to the King in person.

The King listened to her from beginning to end, and then remarked, "You refused the Kings of Denmark, Portugal, Spain, and England, and you wish to marry my captain of the guard, the Marquis de Lauzun?"

"Yes, Sire, for I place him above all monarchs,—yourself alone excepted."

"Do you love him immensely?"

"More than I can possibly say; a thousand, a hundred thousand times more than myself."

"Do you think he is equally devoted to you?"—"That would be impossible," she tranquilly answered; "but his love for me is delicate, tender; and such friendship suffices me."

"My cousin, in all that there is self-interest. I entreat you to reflect. The world, as you know, is a mocking world; you want to excite universal derision and injure the respect which is due to the place that I fill."

"Ah, Sire, do not wound me! I fling myself at your feet. Have compassion upon M. de Lauzun, and pity my tears. Do not exercise your power; let him be the consolation of my life; let me marry him."

The King, no longer able to hide his disgust and impatience, said, "Cousin, you are now a good forty-four years old; at that age you ought to be able to take care of yourself. Spare me all your grievances, and do what pleases you."

On leaving Mademoiselle, he came to my apartment and told me about all this nonsense. I then informed him of what I had heard by letter the day before. Lauzun, while still carrying on with the fastest ladies of the Court and the town, had just wheedled the Princess into making him a present of twenty millions,—a most extravagant gift.

"This is too much!" exclaimed the King; and he at once caused a letter to be despatched to Mademoiselle and her lover, telling them that their intimacy must cease, and that things must go no farther.

But the audacious Lauzun found means to suborn a well-meaning simpleton of a priest, who married them secretly the very same day.

The King's indignation and resentment may well be imagined. He had his captain of the guard arrested and sent as a prisoner to Pignerol.

On this occasion, M. de Lauzun complained bitterly of me; he invented the most absurd tales about me, even saying that he had struck me in my own apartments, after taunting me to my face with "our old intimacy."

That is false; he reproached me with nothing, for there was nothing to reproach. Shortly after the Princess's grand scene, he came and begged me to intercede on his behalf. I only made a sort of vague promise, and he knew well enough that, in the great world, a vague promise is the same as a refusal.

For more than six months I had to stanch the tears and assuage the grief of Mademoiselle. So tiresome to me did this prove, that she alone well-nigh sufficed to make me quit the Court.

Such sorrowing and chagrin made her lose the little beauty that still remained to her; nothing seemed more incongruous and ridiculous than to hear this elderly grand lady talking perpetually about "her dearest darling, the prisoner."

At the time I write he is at Pignerol; his bad disposition is forever getting him into trouble. She sends him lots of money unknown to the King, who generally knows everything. All this money he squanders or gambles away, and when funds are low, says, "The old lady will send us some."

CHAPTER XXXVI.

Hyde, the Chancellor. — Misfortune Not Always Misfortune. — Prince
Comnenus. — The King at Petit-Bourg. — His Incognito. — Who M. de Vivonne
Really Was.

The castle of Petit-Bourg, of which the King made me a present, is situate on a height overlooking the Seine, whence one may get the loveliest of views. So pleasant did I find this charming abode, that I repaired thither as often as possible, and stayed for five or six days. One balmy summer night, I sat in my dressing-gown at the central balcony, watching the stars, as was my wont, asking myself whether I should not be a thousand times happier if I should pass my life in a retreat like this, and so have time to contemplate the glorious works of Nature, and to prepare myself for that separation which sooner or later awaited me. Reason bade me encourage such thoughts, yet my heart offered opposition thereto, urging that there was something terrifying in solitude, most of all here, amid vast fields and meadows, and that, away from the Court and all my friends, I should grow old, and death would take me before my time. While plunged in such thoughts, I suddenly heard the sound of a tocsin, and scanning the horizon, I saw flames and smoke rising from some hamlet or country-house. I rang for my servants, and told them instantly to despatch horsemen to the scene of the catastrophe, and bring back news.

The messengers started off, and soon came back to say that the fire had broken out at the residence of my lord Hyde, Chancellor of England, who was but lately convalescent. They had seen him lying upon a rug on the grass, some little distance from the burning mansion. I forthwith ordered my carriage to be sent for him, and charged my surgeon and secretary to invite him to take shelter at my castle.

My lord gratefully accepted the invitation; he entered my room as the clock struck twelve. As yet he could not tell the cause of the disaster, and in a calm, patriarchal manner observed, "I am a man marked out for great misfortune. God forbid, madame, that the mischance which dogs my footsteps touch you also!"

"I cannot bear to see a fire," said I, in reply to the English nobleman, "for some dreadful accident always results therefrom. Yet, on the whole, they are of good augury, and I am sure, my lord, that your health or your affairs will benefit by this accident."

Hearing me talk thus, my lord smiled. He only took some slight refreshment, — a little soup, — and heard me give orders for all my available servants to be sent to the scene of disaster, in order to save all his furniture, and protect it as well.

After repeated expressions of his gratitude, he desired to withdraw, and retired to rest. Next day we learnt that the fire had been got under about one o'clock in the morning; one wing only of the chateau had been destroyed, and the library, together with all the linen and plate, was well-nigh intact. Lord Hyde was very glad to hear the news. They told him that all the labourers living near had gladly come to the help of his servants and mine. As his private cashbox had been saved, owing to their vigilance and honesty, he promised to distribute its contents among them when he returned.

Hardly had he got the words out, when they came to tell me that, on the highroad, just in front of my gates, a carriage, bound for Paris, had the traces broken, and the travellers persons of distinction begged the favour of my hospitality for a short while. I consented with pleasure, and they went back to take the travellers my answer.

"You see, madame," said the Chancellor, "my bad luck is contagious; no sooner have I set foot in this enchanting abode than its atmosphere deteriorates. A travelling-carriage passes rapidly by in front of the gates, when lo! some invisible hand breaks it to pieces, and stops it from proceeding any further."

Then I replied, "But how do you know, monsieur, that this mishap may not prove a most agreeable adventure for the travellers to whom we are about to give shelter? To begin with, they will have the honour of making your acquaintance, and to meet with an illustrious person is no common or frivolous event."

The servants announced the Princes Comnenus, who immediately entered the salon. Though dressed in travelling-costume, with embroidered gaiters, in the Greek fashion, it was easy to see what they were. The son, a lad of fourteen, was presented to me by his father, and when both were seated, I introduced them to the Chancellor.

"The name is well known," observed the Prince, "even in Greece. My lord married his daughter to the heir-presumptive to the English throne, and England, being by nature ungrateful, has distressed this worthy parent, while robbing him of all his possessions."

At these words Lord Hyde became greatly affected; he could not restrain his tears, and fearing at first to compromise himself, he told us that his exile was voluntary and self-imposed, or very nearly so.

After complimenting the Chancellor of a great kingdom, Prince Comnenus thought that he ought to say something courteous and flattering to myself.

"Madame," quoth he, "it is only now, after asking for hospitality and generously obtaining it, that I and my son have learnt the name of the lady who has so graciously granted us admission to this most lovely place. For a moment we hesitated in awe. But now our eyes behold her whom all Europe admires, whom a great King favours with his friendship and confidence. What strange chances befall one in life! Could I ever have foreseen so fortunate a mishap!"

I briefly replied to this amiable speech, and invited the travellers to spend, at least, one day with us. They gladly accepted, and each retired to his apartment until the time came for driving out. Dinner was laid, and on the point of being served, when the King, who was on his way from Fontainebleau, suddenly entered my room. He had heard something about a fire, and came to see what had happened. I at once informed him, telling him, moreover, that I had the Duke of York's father-in-law staying with me at the moment.

"Lord Hyde, the Chancellor?" exclaimed the King. "I have never seen him, and have always been desirous to make his acquaintance. The opportunity is an easy and favourable one."

"But that is not all, Sire; I have other guests to meet you," said I.

"And who may they be?" inquired the King, smiling. "Just because I have come in rough-and-ready plight, your house is full of people."

"But they are in rough-and-ready plight as well," I answered; "so your
Majesties must mutually excuse each other."

"Are you in fun or in earnest?" asked his Majesty. "Have you really got some king stowed away in one of your rooms?"

"Not a king, Sire, but an emperor, — the Emperor of Constantinople and Trebizond, accompanied by the Prince Imperial, his son. You shall see two Greek profiles of the best sort, two finely cut noses, albeit hooked, and almond-shaped eyes, like those of Achilles and Agamemnon."

Then the King said, "Send for your groom of the chambers at once, and tell him to give orders that my incognito be strictly observed. You must introduce me to these dignitaries as your brother, M. de Vivonne. Under these conditions, I will join your party at table; otherwise, I should be obliged to leave the castle immediately."

The King's wishes were promptly complied with; the footmen were let into the secret, and I introduced "Monsieur de Vivonne" to my guests.

The talk, without being sparkling, was pleasant enough until dessert. When the men-servants left us, it assumed a very different character. The King induced the Chancellor to converse, and asked him if his exile were owing to the English monarch personally, or to some parliamentary intrigue.

"King Charles," replied his lordship, "is a prince to gauge whose character requires long study. Apparently, he is the very soul of candour, but no one is more deceitful than he. He fawns and smiles upon you when in his heart of hearts he despises and loathe you. When the Duke of York, unfortunately, became violently enamoured of my daughter, he did not conceal his attachment from his brother, the King, and at last asked for his approval to join his fortunes to my daughter's, when the King, without offering opposition, contented himself by pointing out the relative distance between their rank and position; to which the Duke replied, 'But at one time you did everything you possibly could to get Olympia Mancini, who was merely Mazarin's niece!' And King Charles, who could not deny this, left his brother complete liberty of action.

"As my daughter was far dearer and more precious to me than social grandeur, I begged the Duke of York to find for himself a partner of exalted rank. He gave way to despair, and spoke of putting an end to his existence; in fact, he behaved as all lovers do whom passion touches to madness; so this baleful marriage took place. God is my witness that I opposed it, urged thereto by wisdom, by modesty, and by foresight. Now, as you see, from that cruel moment I have been exiled to alien lands, robbed of the sight of my beloved child, who has been raised to the rank of a princess, and whom I shall never see again. Why did my sovereign not say to me frankly, I do not like this marriage; you must oppose it, Chancellor, to please me?

"How different was his conduct from that of his cousin, the French King! Mademoiselle d'Orleans wanted to make an unsuitable match; the King opposed it, as he had a right to do, and the marriage did not take place."

My "brother," the King, smiled as he told his lordship he was right.

Prince Comnenus was of the same opinion, and, being expressly invited to do so, he briefly recounted his adventures, and stated the object of his journey to Paris.

"The whole world," said he, "is aware of the great misfortunes of my family. The Emperors Andronicus and Michael Comnenus, driven from the throne of Constantinople, left their names within the heart and memory of Greece; they had ruled the West with a gentle sceptre, and in a people's grateful remembrance they had their reward. My ancestors, their descendants, held sway in Trebizond, a quicksand which gave way beneath their tread. From adversity to adversity, from country to country, we were finally driven to seclusion in the Isle of Candia, part of the quondam Minos territory. Venice had allowed Candia to fall before Mahomet's bloody sword. Europe lost her bulwark, the Cross of the Saviour was thrown down, and the Candian Christians have been massacred or forced to flee. I have left in the hands of the conqueror my fields and forests, my summer palace, my winter palace, and my gardens filled with the produce of America, Asia, and Europe. From this overwhelming disaster I managed to save my son; and as my sole fortune I brought away with me the large jewels of Andronicus, his ivory and sapphire sceptre, his scimitar of Lemnos, and his ancient gold crown, which once encircled Theseus's brow.

"These noble relics I shall present to the King of France. They say that he is humane, generous, fond of glory, and zealous in the cause of justice. When before his now immovable throne he sees laid down these last relics of an ancient race, perhaps he will be touched by so lamentable a downfall, and will not suffer distress to trouble my last days, and darken the early years of this my child."

During this speech I kept watching the King's face. I saw that he was interested, then touched, and at last was on the point of forgetting his incognito and of appearing in his true character.

"Prince," said he to the Greek traveller, "my duties and my devotion make it easy for me to approach the King of France's person very closely. In four or five days he will be leaving Fontainebleau for his palace at Saint Germain. I will tell him without modification all that I have just heard from you. Without being either prophet or seer, I can guarantee that you will be well received and cordially welcomed, receiving such benefits as kings are bound to yield to kings.

"Madame, who respects and is interested in you, is desirous, I feel certain, for me to persuade you to stay here until her departure; she enjoys royal favour, and it is my sister herself who shall present you at Court. You shall show her, you shall show us all, the golden crown of Theseus, the sceptre of Adronicus, and this brow which I gaze upon and revere, for it deserves a kingly diamond.

"As for you, my lord," said his Majesty to the English nobleman, "if the misfortune of last night prove disastrous in more ways than one, pray wait for a while before you go back to the smouldering ashes of a half-extinguished fire. My sister takes pleasure in your company; indeed, the Marquise is charmed to be able to entertain three such distinguished guests, and begs to place her chateau at your disposal until such time as your own shall be restored. We shall speak of you to the King, and he will certainly endeavour to induce King Charles, his cousin, to recall you to your native country."

Then, after saying one or two words to me in private, he bowed to the gentlemen and withdrew. We went out on to the balcony to see him get into his coach, when, to the surprise and astonishment of my guests, as the carriage passed along the avenue, about a hundred peasants, grouped near the gateway, threw off their hats and cried, "Long live the King!"

Prince Comnenus and his son were inconsolable; I excused myself by saying that it was at the express desire of our royal visitor, and my lord admitted that at last he recollected his features, and recognised him by his grand and courtly address.

Before I end my tale, do not let me forget to say that the King strongly recommended Prince Comnenus to the Republic of Genoa, and obtained for him considerable property in Corsica and a handsome residence at Ajaccio. He accepted five or six beautiful jewels that had belonged to Andronicus, and caused the sum of twelve hundred thousand francs to be paid to the young Comnenus from his treasury.

CHAPTER XXXVII

The Universal Jubilee.—Court Preachers.—King David.—Madame de Montespan is Obliged to go to Clagny.—Bossuet's Mission.—Mademoiselle de Mauleon.—An Enemy's Good Faith.

I do not desire to hold up to ridicule the rites of that religion in which I was born and bred. Neither would I disparage its ancient usages, nor its far more modern laws. All religions, as I know, have their peculiarities, all nations their contradictions, but I must be suffered to complain of the abuse sometimes made in our country of clerical and priestly authority.

A general jubilee was held soon after the birth of my second son, and among Christian nations like ours, a jubilee is as if one said, "Now all statutes, divine and earthly, are repealed; by means of certain formula recited, certain visits paid to the temples, certain acts of abstinence practised here and there, all sins, misdemeanours, and crimes are forgiven, and their punishment cancelled." It is generally on the occasion of the proclamation of a new pontificate at Rome that such great papal absolutions are extended over the whole universe.

The jubilee having been proclaimed in Paris, the Court preachers worked miracles. They denounced all social irregularities and friendships of which the Church disapproved. The opening sermon showed plainly that the orator's eloquence was pointed at myself. The second preacher showed even less restraint; he almost mentioned me by name. The third ecclesiastic went beyond all bounds, actually uttering the following words:

"Sire, when King David was still but a shepherd, a heifer was stolen from his flocks; David made complaint to the patriarch of the land, when his heifer was restored to him, and the thief was punished.

"When David came to the throne, he carried off his servant's wife, and as an excuse for such an odious deed, he pleaded the young woman's extreme beauty. The wretched servant besought him to obey the voice, not of passion, but of justice, and the servant was disgraced and perished miserably. Oh, David, unhappy David!"

The King, who had found it hard to sit quiet and hear such insults, said to me that evening:

"Go to Clagny. Let this stormy weather pass by. When it is fine again, you must come back."

Having never run counter to the wishes of the father of my children, I acquiesced, and without further delay gladly departed.

Next day, Madame de Montausier came to see me at my country-house; she told me of the general rumour that was afloat at Court. The news, said she, of my retirement had begun to get about; three bishops had gone to congratulate the King, and these gentlemen had despatched couriers to Paris to inform the heads of the various parishes, inviting them to write to the prince sympathising references touching an event which God and all Christendom viewed with complete satisfaction.

Madame de Montausier assured me that the King's bearing was fairly calm on the whole, and she also added that he had granted an interview of half an hour at least to the Abbe Bossuet, who had discoursed to him about me in a strain similar to that of the other clerics.

She was my sincere friend; she promised to come to Clagny every evening, driving thither incognito.

She had hardly been gone an hour, when my footman announced "Monsieur
Bossuet, Bishop of Condom."

At the mention of this name, I felt momentarily inclined to refuse to see its owner; but I conquered my disgust, and I did well. The prelate, with his semi-clerical, semi-courtly air, made me a low bow. I calmly waited, so as to give him time to deliver his message. The famous rhetorician proceeded as follows:

"You know, madame, with what health-giving sacrifices the Church is now engaged. The merits of our Lord doubtless protect Christians at all times, but the Church has appointed times more efficacious, ceremonies more useful, springs yet more abounding. Thus it is that we now celebrate the grand nine days of the jubilee.

"To this mystic pool herdsman and monarchs alike receive summons and admission. The most Christian King must, for his own sake, accomplish his own sanctification; his sanctification provides for that of his subjects.

"Chosen by God to this royal priesthood, he comprehends the duties imposed upon him by such noble office. The passions of the heart are maladies from which man may recover, just as he recovers from physical disease. The physicians of the soul have lifted up their voice, have taken sage counsel together; and I come to inform you of the monarch's miraculous recovery, and at his request, I bring you this important and welcome news.

"For convalescents, greater care is required than for others; the King, and the whole of France, beseech you, with my voice, to have respect and care for the convalescence of our monarch, and I beg you, madame, to leave at once for Fontevrault."

"For Fontevrault?" I cried, without betraying my emotion. "Fontevrault is near Poitiers; it is too far away. No, I would rather go to Petit-Bourg, near the forest of Fontainebleau."

"Fontainebleau is but eighteen leagues from the capital," he answered; "such proximity would be dangerous. I must insist upon Fontevrault, madame."

"But I cannot take my children to Fontevrault," I retorted; "the nuns, and the Abbess herself, would never admit them. You know better than I do that it is a nunnery."

"Your children," said he, "are not necessary to you; Madame de la Valliere managed to leave here for good and all."

"Yes; and in forsaking them she committed a crime," I answered; "only ferocious-hearted persons could have counselled her or commanded her to do so." And saying this, I rose, and gave him a glance of disdain.

He grew somewhat gentler in manner as he slowly went on, "His Majesty will take care of your children; it behoves you to save their mother. And, in order to prove to you that I have not come here of my own accord, but that, on the contrary, I am executing a formal command, here is a letter of farewell addressed to you by the King."

I took the letter, which was couched in the following terms:

It is but right, madame, that on so solemn an occasion I should set an example myself. I must ask you henceforth to consider our intimacy entirely at an end. You must retire to Fontevrault, where Madame de Montemart will take care of you and afford you distraction by her charming society. Your children are in good hands; do not be in the least uneasy about them. Farewell. I wish you all the firmness and well-being possible. LOUISON.

In the first flush of my indignation I was about to trample under foot so offensive a communication. But the final phrase shocked me less than the others.

I read it over again, and understood that if the King recommended me to be firm, it was because he needed to be firm himself. I soon mastered my emotion, and looked at things in their real light. It was easy to see that sanctimonious fanatics had forced the King to act. Bossuet was not sanctimonious, but, to serve his own ends, proffered himself as spokesman and emissary, being anxious to prove to his old colleagues that he was on the side of what they styled moral conduct and good example.

For a while I walked up and down my salon; but the least exertion fatigues me. I resumed my armchair or my settee, leaving the man there like a sort of messenger, whom it was not necessary to treat with any respect. He was bold, and asked me for a definite answer which he could take back to his Majesty. I stared hard at him for about a minute, and then said: "My Lord Bishop of Condom, the clerics who have been advising the King are very pleased that he should set an example to his people of self-sacrifice. I am of their opinion; I think as they do, as you do, as the Pope does; but feeling convinced that to us, the innocent sheep, the shepherds ought first to show an example, I will consent to break off my relationship with his Majesty when you, M. de Condom, shall have broken off your intimacy with Mademoiselle de Mauleon des Vieux!"

By a retort of this kind I admit that I hoped greatly to embarrass the Bishop, and enjoy seeing his face redden with confusion. But he was nowise disconcerted, and I confess to-day that this circumstance proved to me that there was but little truth in the rumours that were current with regard to this subject.

"Mademoiselle de Mauleon!" said he, smiling half-bitterly, half-pityingly. "Surely, madame, your grief makes you forget what you say. Everybody knows that she is an acquaintance of my youth, and that, since that time, having confidence in my doctrines and my counsel, she wished to have me as spiritual monitor and guide. How can you institute a comparison between such a relationship and your own?" Then, after walking up and down for a moment, as if endeavouring to regain his self-possession, he continued:

"However, I shall not insist further; it was signally foolish of me to speak in the name of an earthly king, when I should have invoked that of the King of Heaven. I have received an insulting answer. So be it.

"Farewell, madame. I leave you to your own conscience, which, seemingly, is so tranquil that I blame myself for having sought to disturb it."

With these words he departed, leaving me much amazed at the patience with which a man, known to be so arrogant and haughty, had received such an onslaught upon his private life and reputation.

I need scarcely say that, next day, the species of pastoral letter which my lords the Bishops of Aleth, Orleans, Soissons, and Condom had dictated to the King was succeeded by another letter, which he had dictated himself, and by which my love for him was solaced and assured.

He begged me to wait patiently for a few days, and this arrangement served my purpose very well. I thought it most amusing that the King should have commissioned M. de Bossuet to deliver this second missive, and I believe I said as much to certain persons, which perhaps gave rise to a rumour that he actually brought me love-letters from the King. But the purveyors of such gossip could surely know nothing of Bossuet's inflexible principles, and of the subtlety of his policy. He was well aware that by lending himself to such amenities he would lose caste morally with the King, and that if by his loyalty he had won royal attachment and regard, all this would have been irretrievably lost. Thus M. de Bossuet was of those who say, "Hate me, but fear me," rather than of those who strive to be loved. Such people know that friendships are generally frail and transient, and that esteem lasts longer and leads further. He never interfered again with my affairs, nor did I with his; I got my way, and he is still where he was.

CHAPTER XXXVIII.

Madame de Montespan Back at Court. — Her Friends. — Her Enemies. — Edifying
Conversions. — The Archbishop of Paris.

Eight days after the conclusion of the jubilee I returned to Versailles. The King received me with every mark of sincere friendship; my friends came in crowds to my apartments; my enemies left their names with my Swiss servant, and in chapel they put back my seat, chairs, and footstools in their usual place.

Madame de Maintenon had twice sent my children to Clagny with the under- governess; but she did not come herself, which greatly inconvenienced me. I complained to her about this, and she assured me the King had dissuaded her from visiting me, "so as to put curious folk off the scent;" and when I told her of my interview with M. de Bossuet, she neatly avoided being mixed up in the matter by omitting to blame anybody. The most licentious women, so she told me, had distinguished themselves by pious exercises during the observance of the jubilee. She informed me that the Comtesse de Soissons, the Princesse de Monaco, Madame de Soubise, and five or six virtuous dames of this type, had given gold, silver, and enamelled lamps to the most notable churches of the capital. The notorious Duchesse de Longueville talked of having her own tomb constructed in a Carmelite chapel. Six leaders of fashion had forsworn rouge, and Madame d'Humieres had given up gambling. As for my lord the Archbishop of Paris, he had not changed his way of life a jot, either for the better or for the worse.

[The splendid Chateau de Clagny (since demolished) was situated on the beautiful country surrounding Versailles, near the wood of Millers d'Avrai. — EDITOR's NOTE.]

CHAPTER XXXIX.

Attempted Abduction. — The Marquise Procures a Bodyguard. —
Her Reasons for
So Doing. — Geography and Morals.

The youthful Marquis d'Antin — my son — was growing up; the King showed him the most flattering signs of his attachment, and as the child had lived only with me, he dreaded his father's violent temper, of which he had often heard me speak. In order to have the custody of his son, the Marquis de Montespan had appealed to Parliament; but partisans of the King had shelved the matter, which, though ever in abeyance, was still pending. I had my son educated under my care, being sure of the tender attachment that would spring up between himself and the princes, his brothers. At the Montespan chateau, I admit, he would have learned to ride an un-broken horse, as well as to shoot hares, partridges, and big game; he would also have learned to talk loud, to use bad language, to babble about his pedigree, while ignorant of its history or its crest; in fine, he would have learned to despise his mother, and probably to hate her. Educated under my eyes, almost on the King's lap, he soon learned the customs of the Court and all that a well-born gentleman should know. He will be made Duc d'Antin, I have the King's word for it, — and his mien and address, which fortunately sort well with that which Fate holds in store for him, entitle him to rank with all that is most exalted at Court.

The Procureur-General caused a man from Barn to be arrested, who had come to abduct my son. This individual, half-Spanish and half-French, was detained in the Paris prisons, and I was left in ignorance of the matter. It was imprudent not to tell me, and almost occasioned a serious mishap.

One day I was returning from the neighbourhood of Etampes with only my son, his tutor, and my physician in the carriage. On reaching a steep incline, where the brake should be put on, my servants imprudently neglected to do this, and I felt that we were burning the roadway in our descent. Such recklessness made me uneasy, when suddenly twelve horsemen rode headlong at us, and sought to stop the postilions. My six horses were new ones and very fresh; they galloped along at breakneck speed. Our pursuers fired at the coachman, but missed him, and the report of a pistol terrified the horses yet further. They redoubled their speed. We gave ourselves up for lost, as an accident of some sort seemed bound to ensue, when suddenly my carriage reached the courtyard of an inn, where we obtained help.

Baulked of their prey, the horsemen turned about and rode away. They had been noticed the day before, hanging about and asking for Madame de Montespan.

We stayed that night at the inn, and next day, provided with a stout escort, we reached Saint Germain.

The King regretted not having provided against similar attempts. He rewarded my postilions for their neglect to use the brake (a neglect which, at first, I was going to punish), saying to me, "If they had put the brake on, you would have been captured and whisked off to the Pyrenees. Your husband is never going to give in!"

"Such a disagreeable surprise," added he, "shall not occur again. Henceforth you shall not travel without an adequate escort. In future, you shall have a guard of honour, like the Queen and myself." I had long wished for this privilege, and I warmly thanked his Majesty.

Nevertheless, people chose to put a completely false construction upon so simple an innovation, and my sentiments in the matter were wholly misunderstood. It was thought that vanity had prompted me to endeavour to put myself on a level with the Queen, and this worthy princess was herself somewhat nettled thereat. God is my witness that, from mere motives of prudence, this unusual arrangement had to be made, and I entirely agreed to it. After all, if the Infanta of Spain gave birth to the Dauphin, Athenais de Mortemart is the mother of several princes.

In France, a Catholic realm, for the King to have a second wife is considered superfluous by the timorous and shrivelled-brained. In Constantinople, Alexandria, and Ispahan, I should have met with only homage, veneration, respect. Errors of a purely geographical nature are not those which cause me alarm; to have brought into the world so perfect a being as the Duc du Maine will never, as I take it, incur blame at the tribunal of Almighty God.

Mademoiselle de Nantes, his charming sister, has from her cradle been destined to belong to one of the royal branches. Mademoiselle de Blois will also become the mother of several Bourbon princes; I have good grounds for cherishing such flattering hopes.

The little Comte de Toulouse already bids fair to be a worthy successor to M. du Maine. He has the same grace of manner, and frank, distinguished mien.

When all these princes possess their several escorts, it will seem passing strange that their mother alone should not have any. That is my opinion, and it is shared by all people of sense.

CHAPTER XL.

Osmin, the Little Moor. — He Sets the Fashion. — The Queen Has a Black
Baby. — Osmin is Dismissed.

I have already told how the envoys of the King of Arda, an African prince, gave to the Queen a nice little blackamoor, as a toy and pet. This Moor, aged about ten or twelve years, was only twenty-seven inches in height, and the King of Arda declared that, being quite unique, the boy would never grow to be taller than three feet.

The Queen instantly took a great fancy to this black creature. Sometimes he gambolled about and turned somersaults on her carpet like a kitten, or frolicked about on the bureau, the sofa, and even on the Queen's lap.

As she passed from one room to another, he used to hold up her train, and delighted to catch hold of it and so make the Queen stop short suddenly, or else to cover his head and face with it, for mischief, to make the courtiers laugh.

He was arrayed in regular African costume, wearing handsome bracelets, armlets, a necklace ablaze with jewels, and a splendid turban. Wishing to show myself agreeable, I gave him a superb aigrette of rubies and diamonds; I was always sorry afterwards that I did so.

The King could never put up with this little dwarf, albeit his features were comely enough. To begin with, he thought him too familiar, and never even answered him when the dwarf dared to address him.

Following the fashion set by her Majesty, all the Court ladies wanted to have little blackamoors to follow them about, set off their white complexions, and hold up their cloaks or their trains. Thus it came that Mignard, Le Bourdon, and other painters of the aristocracy, used to introduce negro boys into all their large portraits. It was a mode, a mania; but so absurd a fashion soon had to disappear after the mishap of which I am about to tell.

The Queen being pregnant, public prayers were offered up for her according to custom, and her Majesty was forever saying: "My pregnancy this time is different from preceding ones. I am a prey to nausea and strange whims; I have never felt like this before. If, for propriety's sake, I did not restrain myself, I should now dearly like to be turning somersaults on the carpet, like little Osmin. He eats green fruit and raw game; that is what I should like to do, too. I should like to—"

"Oh, madame, you frighten us!" exclaimed the King. "Don't let all those whimsies trouble you further, or you will give birth to some monstrosity, some freak of nature." His Majesty was a true prophet. The Queen was delivered of a fine little girl, black as ink from head to foot. They did not tell her this at once, fearing a catastrophe, but persuaded her to go to sleep, saying that the child had been taken away to be christened.

The physicians met in one room, the bishops and chaplains in another. One prelate was opposed to baptising the infant; another only agreed to this upon certain conditions. The majority decided that it should be baptised without the name of father or mother, and such suppression was unanimously advocated.

The little thing, despite its swarthy hue, was most beautifully made; its features bore none of those marks peculiar to people of colour.

It was sent away to the Gisors district to be suckled as a negro's daughter, and the Gazette de France contained an announcement to the effect that the royal infant had died, after having been baptised by the chaplains.

[This daughter of the Queen lived, and was obliged to enter a Benedictine nunnery at Moret. Her portrait is to be seen in the Sainte Genevieve Library of Henri IV.'s College, where it hangs in the winter saloon.—EDITOR'S NOTE.]

The little African was sent away, as may well be imagined; and the Queen admitted that, one day soon after she was pregnant, he had hidden himself behind a piece of furniture and suddenly jumped out upon her to give her a fright. In this he was but too successful.

The Court ladies no longer dared come near the Queen attended by their little blackamoors. These, however, they kept for a while longer, as if they were mere nick-hacks or ornaments; in Paris they were still to be seen in public. But the ladies' husbands at last got wind of the tale, when all the little negroes disappeared.

CHAPTER XLI.

Monsieur's Second Marriage. — Princess Palatine. — The Court Turnspit. — A Woman's Hatred. — The King's Mistress on a Par with the First Prince of the Blood. — She Gives His Wife a Lesson.

In order to keep up appearances at his Palais Royal, Monsieur besought the King to consent to his remarriage after the usual term of mourning was at an end.

"Whom have you in view?" asked his brother. He replied that he proposed to wed Mademoiselle — the grande Mademoiselle de Montpensier — on account of her enormous wealth!

Just then Mademoiselle was head over ears in love with Lauzun. She sent the Prince about his business, as I believe I have already stated. Moreover, she remarked: "You had the loveliest wife in all Europe, — young, charming, a veritable picture. You might have seen to it that she was not poisoned; in that case you would not now be a widower. As it is not likely that I should ever come to terms with your favourites, I shall never be anything else to you but a cousin, and I shall endeavour not to die until the proper time; that is, when it shall please God to take me. You can repeat this speech, word for word, to your precious Marquis d'Effiat and Messieurs de Remecourt and de Lorraine. They have no access to my kitchens; I am not afraid of them."

This answer amused the King not a little, and he said to me: "I was told that the Palatine of Bavaria's daughter is extremely ugly and ill-bred; consequently, she is capable of keeping Monsieur in check. Through one of my Rhenish allies, I will make proposals to her father for her hand. As soon as a reply comes, I will show my brother a portrait of some sort; it will be all the same to him; he will accept her."

Soon afterwards this marriage took place. Charlotte Elizabeth of Bavaria, though aware of the sort of death that her predecessor died, agreed to marry Monsieur. Had she not been lucky enough to make this grand match, her extreme ugliness would assuredly have doomed her to celibacy, even in Bavaria and in Germany. It is surely not allowable to come into the world with such a face and form, such a voice, such eyes, such hands, and such feet, as this singular princess displayed. The Court, still mindful of the sweetness, grace, and charm of Henrietta of England, could not contemplate without horror and disgust the fearful caricature I have just described. Young pregnant women—after the Queen's unfortunate experience—were afraid to look at the Princess Palatine, and wished to be confined before they reappeared at Court.

As for herself, armed with robust, philosophical notions, and a complete set of Northern nerves, she was in no way disconcerted at the effect her presence produced. She even had the good sense to appear indifferent to all the raillery she provoked, and said to the King:

"Sire, to my mind you are one of the handsomest men in the world, and with few exceptions, your Court appears to me perfectly fitted for you. I have come but scantily equipped to such an assemblage. Fortunately, I am neither jealous nor a coquette, and I shall win pardon for my plainness, I myself being the first to make merry at it."

"You put us completely at our ease," replied the King, who had not even the courage to be gallant. "I must thank you on behalf of these ladies for your candour and wit." Ten or twelve of us began to titter at this speech of hers. The Robust Lady never forgave those who laughed.

Directly she arrived, she singled me out as the object of her ponderous Palatine sarcasms. She exaggerated my style of dress, my ways and habits. She thought to make fun of my little spaniels by causing herself to be followed, even into the King's presence-chamber, by a large turnspit, which in mockery she called by the name of my favourite dog.

When I had had my hair dressed, ornamented with quantities of little curls, diamonds, and jewelled pins, she had the impertinence to appear at Court wearing a huge wig, a grotesque travesty of my coiffure. I was told of it. I entered the King's apartment without deigning to salute Madame, or even to look at her.

I had also been told that, in society, she referred to me as "the Montespan woman." I met her one day in company with a good many other people, and said to her:

"Madame, you managed to give up your religion in order to marry a French prince; you might just as well have left behind your gross Palatine vulgarity also. I have the honour to inform you that, in the exalted society to which you have been admitted, one can no more say 'the Montespan woman,' than one can say 'the Orleans woman.' I have never offended you in the slightest degree, and I fail to see why I should have been chosen as the favoured object of your vulgar insults."

She blushed, and ventured to inform me that this way of expressing herself was a turn of speech taken from her own native language, and that by saying "the," as a matter of course "Marquise" was understood.

"No, madame," I said, without appearing irritated; "in Paris, such an excuse as that is quite inadmissible, and since you associate with turnspits, pray ask your cooks, and they will tell you."

Fearing to quarrel with the King, she was obliged to be more careful, but to change one's disposition is impossible, and she has loathed and insulted me ever since. Her husband, who himself probably taught her to do so, one day tried to make apologies for what he ruefully termed her reprehensible conduct. "There, there, it doesn't matter," I said to him; "it is easier to offend me than to deceive me. Allow me to quote to you the speech of Mademoiselle de Montpensier, 'You had a charming and accomplished wife, you ought to have prevented her from being poisoned, and then we should not have had this hag at Court.'"

CHAPTER XLII.

Madame de Montespan's Father-confessor. — He Alters His Opinion. — Madame de Maintenon Is Consulted. — A General on Theolo-
gy. — A Country Priest. — The Marquise Postpones Her Repentance
and Her Absolution.

My father-confessor, who since my arrival at Court had never
vexed or thwarted me, suddenly altered his whole manner towards
me, from which I readily concluded that the Queen had got hold of
him. This priest, of gentle, easy-going, kindly nature, never spoke to
me except in a tone of discontent and reproach. He sought to induce
me to leave the King there and then, and retire to some remote chateau. Seeing that he was intriguing, and had, so to speak, taken up
his position, like a woman of experience I took up mine as well, and
politely dismissed him, at which he was somewhat surprised. In
matters of religion, Madame de Maintenon, who understands such
things, was my usual mentor. I told her that I was disheartened, and
should not go to confession again for ever so long. She was shocked
at my resolve, and strove all she could to make me change my mind
and endeavour to lead me back into the right way.

She forever kept repeating her favourite argument, saying, "Good
gracious! suppose you should die in that state!"

I replied that it was not my fault, as I had never ceased to obey
the precepts of the Holy Church. "It was my old father-confessor,"
said I, "the Canon of Saint Thomas du Louvre, who had harshly
refused to confess me."

"What he does," replied she, "is solely for your own good."

"But if he has only my well-being in view," I quickly retorted,
"why did not he think of this at first? It would have been far better
to have stopped me at the outset, instead of letting me calmly pro-
ceed upon my career. He is obeying the Queen's orders, or else

those of that Abbe Bossuet de Mauleon, who no longer dares attack me to my face."

As we thus talked, the Duc de Vivonne came into my room. Learning the topic of our discussion, he spoke as follows: "I should not be general of the King's Galleys and a soldier at heart and by profession if my opinion in this matter were other than it is. I have attentively read controversies on this point, and have seen it conclusively proved that our kings never kept a confessor at Court. Among these kings, too, there were most holy, most saintly people, and—"

"Then, what do you conclude from that, Duke?" asked Madame de Maintenon.

"Why, that Madame will do well to respect his Majesty the King as her father-confessor."

"Oh, Duke, you shock me! What dreadful advice, to be sure!" cried the governess.

"I have not the least wish to shock you, madame; but my veneration for D'Aubigne—your illustrious grandfather—is too great to let me think that he is among the damned, and he never attended confession at all."

[Theodore Agrippa, Baron d'Aubigne, lieutenant-general in the army of
Henri IV. He persevered in Calvinism after the recantation of the King.—EDITOR'S NOTE.]

"Eternity hides that secret from us," replied Madame de Maintenon. "Each day I pray to God to have mercy upon my poor grandfather; if I thought he were among the saved, I should never be at pains to do this."

"Bah, madame! let's talk like sensible, straightforward people," quoth the General. "The reverend Pere de la Chaise—one of the Jesuit oracles—gives the King absolution every year, and authorises him to receive the Holy Sacrament at Easter. If the King's confessor—thorough priest as he is—pardons his intimacy with madame, here, how comes it that the other cleric won't tolerate madame's intimacy with the King? On a point of such importance as this, the two confessors ought really to come to some agreement, or else, as the Jesuits have such a tremendous reputation, the Marquise is entitled to side with them."

Hemmed in thus, Madame de Maintenon remarked "that the morals of Jesuits and lax casuists had never been hers," and she advised me to choose a confessor far removed from the Court and its intrigues.

The next day she mentioned a certain village priest to me, uninfluenced by anybody, and whose primitive simplicity caused him to be looked upon as a saint.

I submitted, and ingenuously went to confess myself to this wonderful man; his great goodness did not prevent him from rallying me about the elegance of my costume, and the perfume of my gloves, and my hair. He insisted upon knowing my name, and on learning it, flew into a passion. I suppress the details of his disagreeable propositions. Seated sideways in his confessional, he stamped on the floor, abused me, and spoke disrespectfully of the King. I could not stand such scandalous behaviour for long; and, wearing my veil down, I got into my coach, being thoroughly determined that I would take a good long holiday. M. de Vivonne soundly rated me for such cowardice, as he called it, while Madame de Maintenon offered me her curate-in-chief, or else the Abbe Gobelin.

But, for the time being, I determined to keep to my plan of not going to confession, strengthened in such resolve by my brother Vivonne's good sense, and the attitude of the King's Jesuit confessor, who had a great reputation and knew what he was about.

CHAPTER XLIII.

The Comte de Guiche. — His Violent Passion for Madame. — His Despair. — He
Flees to La Trappe. — And Comes Out Again. — A Man's Heart. — Cured of His
Passion, He Takes a Wife.

The Comte de Guiche, son of the Marechal de Grammont, was undoubtedly one of the handsomest men in France.

The grandeur and wealth of his family had, at an early age, inspired him with courage and self-conceit, so that in his blind, frivolous presumption, the only person, as he thought, who exceeded his own fascination was possibly the King, but nobody else.

Perceiving the wonderful charm of Monsieur's first wife, he conceived so violent a passion for her that no counsel nor restraint could prevent him from going to the most extravagant lengths in obedience to this rash, this boundless passion.

Henrietta of England, much neglected by her husband, and naturally of a romantic disposition, allowed the young Count to declare his love for her, either by singing pretty romances under her balcony, or by wearing ribbons, bunched together in the form of a hieroglyphic, next his heart. Elegantly dressed, he never failed to attend all the assemblies to which she lent lustre by her presence. He followed her to Saint Germain, to Versailles, to Chambord, to Saint Cloud; he only lived and had his being in the enjoyment of contemplating her charms.

One day, being desirous of walking alongside her sedan-chair, without being recognised, he had a complete suit made for him of the La Valliere livery, and thus, seeming to be one of the Duchess's pages, he was able to converse with Madame for a short time. Another time he disguised himself as a pretty gipsy, and came to tell the Princess her fortune. At first she did not recognise him, but when the secret was out, and all the ladies were in fits of laughter, a page came running in to announce the arrival of Monsieur. Young De Guiche slipped out by a back staircase, and in order to facilitate his exit, one of the footmen, worthy of Moliere, caught hold of the Prince as if he were one of his comrades, and holding a handkerchief over his face, nearly poked his eye out.

The Count's indiscretions were retailed in due course to Monsieur by his favourites, and he was incensed beyond measure. He complained to Marechal de Grammont; he complained to the King.

Hereupon, M. de Guiche received orders to travel for two or three years.

War with the Turks had just been declared, and together with other officers, his friends, he set out for Candia and took part in the siege. All did him the justice to affirm that while there he behaved like a hero. When the fortress had to capitulate, and Candia was lost to the Christians forever, our officers returned to France. Madame was still alive when the young Count rejoined his family. He met the Princess once or twice in society, without being able to approach her person, or say a single word to her.

Soon afterwards, she gave birth to a daughter. A few days later, certain monsters took her life by giving her poison. This dreadful event made such an impression upon the poor Comte de Guiche, that for a long while he lost his gaiety, youth, good looks, and to a certain extent, his reason. After yielding to violent despair, he was possessed with rash ideas of vengeance. The Marechal de Grammont had to send him away to one of his estates, for the Count talked of attacking and of killing, without further ado, the Marquis d'Effiat, M. de Remecourt, the Prince's intendant, named Morel, and even the Duc d'Orleans himself.

[Morel subsequently admitted his guilt in the matter of Madame's death, as well as the commission of other corresponding crimes. See the Letters of Charlotte, the Princess Palatine. — EDITOR'S NOTE.]

His intense agitation was succeeded by profound melancholy, stupor closely allied to insanity or death.

One evening, the Comte de Guiche went to the Abbey Church of Saint Denis. He hid himself here, to avoid being watched, and when the huge nave was closed, and all the attendants had left, he rushed forward and flung himself at full length upon the tombstone which covers the vast royal vault. By the flickering light of the lamps, he mourned the passing hence of so accomplished a woman, murdered in the flower of her youth. He called her by name, telling her once more of his deep and fervent love. Next day, he wandered about in great pain, gloomy and inconsolable.

One day he came to see me at Clagny, and talked in a hopeless, desolate way about our dear one. He told me that neither glory nor ambition nor voluptuous pleasures could ever allure him or prove soothing to his soul. He assured me that life was a burden to him,— a burden that religion alone prevented him from relinquishing, and that he was determined to shut himself up in La Trappe or in some such wild, deserted place.

I sought to dissuade him from such a project, which could only be the cause of grief and consternation to his relatives. He pretended to yield to my entreaties, but the next night he left home and disappeared.

At length he came back. Luckily, the Trappist Abbe de Ranch wished to take away from him the portrait on enamel of Henrietta of England, so as to break it in pieces before his eyes. So indignant was the Count that he was upon the point of giving the hermit a thrashing. He fled in disgust from the monastery, and this fresh annoyance served, in some degree, to assuage his grief. Life's daily occupations, the excitements of society, the continual care shown towards him by his relatives, youth, above all, and Time, the irresistible healer, at last served to soothe a sorrow which, had it lasted longer, would have been more disastrous in its results.

The Comte de Guiche consented to marry a wife to whom he was but slightly attached, and who is quite content with him, praising his good qualities and all his actions.

CHAPTER XLIV.

Mexica. — Philippa. — Molina. — The Queen's Jester.

In marrying Maria Theresa, Infanta of Spain, the King had made an advantageous match from a political point of view. For through the Infanta he had rights with regard to Flanders; she also provided him with eventual claims upon Spain itself, together with Mexico and Peru. But from a personal and social point of view, the King could not have contracted a more miserable alliance. The Infanta, almost wholly uneducated, had not even such intellectual resources as a position such as hers certainly required, where personal risk was perpetual, where authority had to be maintained by charming manners, and respect for power ensured by elevation of tone and sentiment, which checks the indiscreet, and imbues everybody with the spirit of consideration and reverence.

Maria Theresa, though a king's daughter, made no more effect at Court than if she had been a mere middle-class person. The King, in fact, by his considerateness, splendour, and glory, served to support her dignity. He hoped and even desired that she should be held in honour, partly for her own sake, in a great measure for his. But as soon as she started upon some argument or narration where force of intellect was needed, she always seemed bewildered, and he soon interrupted her either by finishing the tale himself, or by changing the conversation. This he did good-naturedly and with much tact, so that the Queen, instead of taking offence, was pleased to be under such an obligation to him. From such a wife this prince could not look to have sons of remarkable talent or intellect, for that would have been nothing short of a miracle. And thus the little Dauphin showed none of those signs of intelligence which the most ordinary commonplace children usually display. When the Queen heard courtiers repeat some of the droll, witty sayings of the Comte de Vegin, or the Duc du Maine, she reddened with jealousy, and remarked, "Everybody goes into ecstasies about those children, while Monsieur le Dauphin is never even mentioned."

She had brought with her from Spain that Donna Silvia Molina, of whom I have already spoken, and who had got complete control over her character. Instead of tranquillising her, and so making her happy, Donna Silvia thought to become more entertaining, and above all, more necessary to her, by gossiping to her about the King's amours. She ferreted out all the secret details, all the petty circumstances, and with such dangerous material troubled the mind and destroyed the repose of her mistress, who wept unceasingly, and became visibly changed.

La Molina, enriched and almost wealthy, was sent back to Spain, much to the grief of Maria Theresa, who for several days after her departure could neither eat nor sleep.

At the same time, the King got rid of that little she-dwarf, named Mexica, in whose insufferable talk and insufferable presence the Queen took delight. But the sly little wretch escaped during the journey, and managed to get back to the princess again, hidden in some box or basket. The Queen was highly delighted to see her again; she pampered her secretly in her private cabinet with the utmost mystery, giving up every moment that she could spare.

One day, by way of a short cut, the King was passing through the Queen's closet, when he heard the sound of coughing in one of the cupboards. Turning back, he flung it open, where, huddled up in great confusion, he found Mexica.

"What!" cried his Majesty; "so you are back again? When and how did you come?"

In a feeble voice Mexica answered, "Sire, please don't send me away from the Queen any more, and she will never complain again about Madame de Montespan."

The King laughed at this speech, and then came and repeated it to me. I laughed heartily, too, and such a treaty of peace seemed to contain queer compensation clauses: Madame de Montespan and Mexica were mutually bound over to support each other; the spectacle was vastly droll, I vow.

Besides her little dwarf, the Queen had a fool named Tricominy. This quaint person was permitted to utter everywhere and to everybody in incoherent fashion the pseudo home-truths that passed through his head. One day he went up to the grande Mademoiselle de Montpensier, and said to her before everybody, "Since you are so anxious to get married, marry me; then that will be a man-fool and a woman-fool." The Princess tried to hit him, and he took refuge behind the Queen's chair.

Another time, to M. Letellier, Louvois's brother and Archbishop of Rheims, he said, "Monseigneur, do let me ascend the pulpit in your Cathedral, and I will preach modesty and humanity to you." When the little Duc d'Anjou, that pretty, charming child, died of suppressed measles, the Queen was inconsolable, and the King, good father that he is, was weeping for the little fellow, for he promised much. Says Tricominy, "They're weeping just as if princes had not got to die like anybody else. M. d'Anjou was no better made than I am, nor of better stuff."

Tricominy was dismissed, because it was plain that his madness took a somewhat eccentric turn; that, in fact, he was not fool enough for his place.

The Queen had still a Spanish girl named Philippa, to whom she was much attached, and who deserved such flattering attachment. Born in the Escurial Palace, Philippa had been found one night in a pretty cradle at the base of one of the pillars. The palace guards informed King Philip, who adopted the child and brought it up, since it had been foisted upon him as his daughter. He grew fond of the girl, and on coming to Saint Jean de Luz to marry the Infanta to his nephew the King, he made them a present of Philippa, and begged them both to be very good to her. In this amiable Spanish girl, the Infanta recognised a sister. She knew she was an illegitimate daughter of King Philip and one of the palace ladies.

When Molina left the Court, she did everything on earth to induce Philippa to return with her to Spain, but the girl was sincerely attached to the Queen, who, holding her in a long embrace, promised to find her a wealthy husband if she would stay. However, the Queen only gave her as husband the Chevalier de Huze, her cloak-bearer, so as to keep the girl about her person and to be intimate with her daily. Philippa played the mandolin and the guitar to perfection; she, also sang and danced with consummate grace.

CHAPTER XLV.

Le Bouthilier de Ranch, Abbe de la Trappe.

The Abbe le Bouthilier de Rance, — son of the secretary of state, Le Bouthilier de Chavigny, — after having scandalised Court and town by his public gallantries, lost his mistress, a lady possessed of a very great name and of no less great beauty. His grief bordered upon despair; he forsook the world, gave away or sold his belongings, and went and shut himself up in his Abbey of La Trappe, the only benefice which he had retained. This most ancient monastery was of the Saint Bernard Order, with white clothing. The edifice spacious, yet somewhat dilapidated was situated on the borders of Normandy, in a wild, gloomy valley exposed to fog and frost.

The Abbe found in this a place exactly suitable to his plan, which was to effect reforms of austere character and contrary to nature. He convened his monks, who were amazed at his arrival and residence; he soundly rated them for the scandalous laxity of their conduct, and having reminded them of all the obligations of their office, he informed them of his new regulations, the nature of which made them tremble. He proposed nothing less than to condemn them to daily manual labour, the tillage of the soil, the performance of menial household duties; and to this he added the practices of immoderate fasting, perpetual silence, downcast glances, veiled countenances, the renouncement of all social ties, and all instructive or entertaining literature. In short, he advocated sleeping all together on the bare floor of an ice-cold dormitory, the continual contemplation of death, the dreadful obligation of digging, while alive, one's own grave every day with one's own hands, and thus, in imagination, burying oneself therein before being at rest there for ever.

As laws so foolish and so tyrannical were read out to them, the worthy monks—all of them of different character and age openly expressed their discontent. The Abbe de Rance allowed them to go and get pleasure in other monasteries, and contrived to collect around him youths whom it was easy to delude, and a few elderly misanthropes; with these he formed his doleful wailing flock.

As he loved notoriety in everything, he had various views of his monastery engraved, and pictures representing the daily pursuits of his laborious community. Such pictures, hawked about everywhere by itinerant vendors of relics and rosaries, served to create for this barbarous reformer a reputation saintly and angelic. In towns, villages, even in royal palaces, he formed the one topic of conversation. Several gentlemen, disgusted either with vice or with society, retired of their own accord to his monastery, where they remained in order that they might the sooner die.

Desirous of enjoying his ridiculous celebrity, the Abbe de Rance came to Paris, under what pretext I do not remember, firmly resolved to show himself off in all the churches, and solicit abundant alms for his phantoms who never touched food. From all sides oblations were forthcoming; soon he had got money enough to build a palace, if he had liked.

It being impossible for him to take the august Mademoiselle de Montpensier to his colony of monks, he desired at any rate to induce her to withdraw from the world, and counselled her to enter a Carmelite convent. Mademoiselle's ardent passion for M. de Lauzun seemed to the Trappist Abbe a scandal; in fact, his sour spirit could brook no scandal of any sort. "I attended her father as he lay dying," said he, "and to me belongs the task of training, enlightening, and sanctifying his daughter. I would have her keep silence; she has spoken too much."

The moment was ill chosen; just then Mademoiselle de Montpensier was striving to break the fetters of her dear De Lauzun; she certainly did not wish to get him out of one prison, and then put herself into another. Every one blamed this reformer's foolish presumption, and Mademoiselle, thoroughly exasperated, forbade her servants to admit him. It was said that he had worked two or three miracles, and brought certain dead people back to life.

"I will rebuild his monastery for him in marble if he will give us back poor little Vegin, and the Duc d'Anjou," said the King to me.

The remark almost brought tears to my eyes, just as I was about to joke with his Majesty about the fellow and his miracles.

Well satisfied with his Parisian harvest, the Abbe le Bouthilier de Rance went straight to his convent, where the inmates were persevering enough to be silent, fast, dig, catch their death of cold, and beat themselves for him.

Madame Cormeil, wishing to have a good look at the man, sent to inform him of her illness. Would-be saints are much afraid of words with a double meaning. In no whit disconcerted, he replied that he had devoted his entire zeal to the poor in spirit, and that Madame Cormeil was not of their number.

CHAPTER XLVI.

Before relating that which I have to say about the Queen and her
precautions against myself, I would not omit certain curious inci-
dents during the journey that the King caused us to take in Alsatia
and Flanders, when he captured Maestricht and Courtrai.

The King having left us behind at Nancy, a splendid town where
a large proportion of the nobility grieved for the loss of Messieurs
de Lorraine, their legitimate sovereigns, the Queen soon saw that
here she was more honoured than beloved. It was this position
which suggested to her the idea of going to Spa, close by, and of
taking the waters for some days.

If the Infanta was anxious to escape from the frigid courtesies of
the Lorraine aristocracy, I also longed to have a short holiday, and
to keep away from the Queen, as well for the sake of her peace of
mind as for my own. My doctor forbade me to take the Spa waters,
as they were too sulphurous; he ordered me those of Pont-a-
Mousson. Hardly had I moved there, when orders came for us all to
meet at Luneville, and thence we set out to rejoin the King.

Horrible was the first night of our journey spent at Ravon, in the
Vosges Mountains. The house in which Mademoiselle de Montpensier and I lodged was a dilapidated cottage, full of holes, and
propped up in several places. Lying in bed, we heard the creaking
of the beams and rafters. Two days afterwards the house, so they
told us, collapsed.

From that place we went on to Sainte Marie aux Mines, a mean sort of town, placed like a long corridor between two lofty, well-wooded mountains, which even at noonday deprive it of sun. Close by there is a shallow, rock-bound streamlet which divides Lorraine from Alsace. Sainte Marie aux Mines belonged to the Prince Palatine of Birkenfeld. This Prince offered us his castle of Reif Auvilliers, an uncommonly beautiful residence, which he had inherited from the Comtesse de Ribaupierre, his wife.

This lady's father was just dead, and as, in accordance with German etiquette, the Count's funeral obsequies could not take place for a month, in the presence of all his relatives and friends, who came from a great distance, the corpse, embalmed and placed in a leaden coffin, lay in state under a canopy in the mortuary chapel.

Our equerries, seeing that the King's chamber looked on to the mortuary chapel, took upon themselves to blow out all the candles, and for the time being stowed away the corpse in a cupboard.

We knew nothing about this; and as the castle contained splendid rooms, the ladies amused themselves by dancing and music to make them forget the boredom of their journey.

The King looked in upon us every now and then, saying, in a low voice,
"Ah! if you only knew what I know!"

And then he would go off, laughing in his sleeve. We did not get to know about this corpse until five or six days afterwards, when we were a long way off, and the discovery greatly shocked us.

The day we left Sainte Marie aux Mines, a little German sovereign came to present his homage to the King. It was the Prince de Mont-Beliard, of Wurtemberg, whom I had previously met in Paris, on the occasion of his marriage with Marechal de Chatillon's charming daughter. The luxurious splendour of Saint Germain and Versailles had certainly not yet succeeded in turning the heads of these German sovereigns. This particular one wore a large buff doublet with big copper-gilt buttons. His cravat was without either ribbons or lace. His rather short hair was roughly combed over his forehead; he carried no sword, and instead of gold buckles or clasps, he had little bows of red leather on his black velvet shoes. His coach, entirely black, was still of old-fashioned make; that is to say, studded with quantities of gilt nails. Wearing mourning for the Empress, his six horses were richly, caparisoned, his four lackeys wearing yellow liveries faced with red. An escort of twenty guardsmen, dressed similarly, was in attendance; they seemed to be well mounted, and were handsome fellows.

A second carriage of prodigious size followed the ducal conveyance; in this were twelve ladies and gentlemen, who got out and made their obeisance to the King and Queen.

The Prince de Mont-Beliard did not get into his coach again until ours were in motion. He spoke French fairly well, and the little he said was said with much grace. He looked very hard at me, which shocked the Queen greatly, but not the King.

A little further on, their Majesties were greeted by the delegates of the noble chapter of Strasburg. These comprised the Count of Manderhall and two canons. What canons, too! And how astonished we were!

The old Count was dressed in a black cassock, and his hair looked somewhat like a cleric's, but his cravat was tied with a large flame-coloured bow, and he wore ill-fitting hose of the same hue. As for the two canons, they were pleasant young men, good-looking and well-made. Their light gray dress was edged with black and gold; they wore their hair long in wavy curls, and in their little black velvet caps they had yellow and black feathers, and their silver-mounted swords were like those worn by our young courtiers. Their equipment was far superior to that of the deputation of the Prince de Mont-Beliard. It is true, they were churchmen, and churchmen have only themselves and their personal satisfaction to consider.

These gentlemen accompanied us as far as Chatenoi, a little town in their neighbourhood, and here they introduced the bailiff of the town to the King, who was to remain constantly in attendance and act as interpreter.

The bailiff spoke French with surprising ease. He had been formerly tutor at President Tambonneaux's, an extremely wealthy man, who entertained the Court, the town, and all the cleverest men of the day. The King soon became friends with the bailiff, and kept him the whole time close to his carriage.

When travelling, the King is quite another man. He puts off his gravity of demeanour, and likes to amuse his companions, or else make his companions amuse him. Believing him to be like Henri IV. in temper, the bailiff was for asking a thousand questions. Some of these the King answered; to others he gave no reply.

"Sire," said he to his Majesty, "your town of Paris has a greater reputation than it actually deserves. They say you are fond of building; then Paris ought to have occasion to remember your reign. Allow me to express a hope that her principal streets will be widened, that her temples, most of them of real beauty, may be isolated. You should add to the number of her bridges, quays, public baths, almshouses and infirmaries."

The King smiled. "Come and see us in four or five years," he rejoined, "or before that, if you like, and if your affairs permit you to do so. You will be pleased to see what I have already done."

Then the bailiff, approaching my carriage window, addressed a few complimentary remarks to myself.

"I have often met your father, M. de Mortemart," said he, "at President
Tambonneaux's. One day the little De Bouillons were there, quarrelling
about his sword, and to the younger he said, 'You, sir, shall go into the
Church, because you squint. Let my sword alone; here's my rosary.'"

"Well," quoth the King, "M. de Mortemart was a true prophet, for that little Bouillon fellow is to-day Cardinal de Bouillon."

"Sire," continued the worthy German, "I am rejoiced to hear such news. And little Peguilain de Lauzun, of whom you used to be so fond when you were both boys,—where is he? What rank does he now hold?"

Hereupon the King looked at Mademoiselle, who, greatly confused, shed tears.

"Well, M. Bailiff," said his Majesty, "did you easily recognise me at first sight?"

"Sire," replied the German, "your physiognomy is precisely the same; when a boy, you looked more serious. The day you entered Parliament in hunting-dress I saw you get into your coach; and that evening the President said to his wife, 'Madame, we are going to have a King. I wish you could have been there, in one of the domes, just to hear the little he said to us.'"

Whereupon the King laughingly inquired what reply the President's wife made. But the bailiff, smiling in his turn, seemed afraid to repeat it, and so his Majesty said:

"I was told of her answer at the time, so I can let you know what it was.
'Your young King will turn out a despot.' That is what Madame la Presidente said to her husband."

The bailiff, somewhat confused, admitted that this was exactly the case.

The huge bridge at Brisach, across the Rhine, had no railing; the planks were in a rickety condition, and through fissures one caught sight of the impetuous rush of waters below. We all got out of our coaches and crossed over with our eyes half shut, so dangerous did it seem; while the King rode across this wretched bridge,—one of the narrowest and loftiest that there is, and which is always in motion.

Next day the Bishop of Bale came to pay his respects to the Queen, and was accompanied by delegates from the Swiss cantons, and other notabilities. After this I heard the "General of the Capucins" announced, who had just been to pay a visit of greeting to the German Court. He was said to be by birth a Roman. Strange to say, for that Capucin the same ceremony and fuss was made as for a sovereign prince, and I heard that this was a time-honoured privilege enjoyed by his Order. The monk himself was a fine man, wearing several decorations; his carriage, livery, and train seemed splendid, nor did he lack ease of manner nor readiness of conversation. He told us that, at the imperial palace in Vienna, he had seen the Princesse d'Inspruck,—a relative of the French Queen, and that the Emperor was bringing her up as if destined one day to be his seventh bride, according to a prediction. He also stated that the Emperor had made the young Princess sing to him,—a Capucin monk; and added genially that she was comely and graceful, and that he had been very pleased to see her.

The King was very merry at this priest's expense. Not so the Queen, who was Spanish, and particularly devoted to Capucin friars of all nationalities.

CHAPTER XLVII.

Moliere. — Racine. — Their Mutual Esteem. — Racine in Mourning.

The King had not much leisure, yet occasionally he gave up half an hour or an hour to the society of a chosen few, — men famous for their wit and brilliant talents. One day he was so kind as to bring to my room the celebrated Moliere, to whom he was particularly attached and showed special favour. "Madame," said the King, "here you see the one man in all France who has most wit, most talent, and most modesty and good sense combined. I thank God for letting him be born during my reign, and I pray that He may preserve him to us for a long while yet."

As I hastened to add my own complimentary remarks to those of the King, I certainly perceived that about this illustrious person there was an air of modesty and simplicity such as one does not commonly find in Apollo's favourites who aspire to fame. Moreover, he was most comely.

Moliere told the King that he had just sketched out the plot of his "Malade Imaginaire," and assured us that hypochondriacs themselves would find something to laugh at when it was played. He spoke very little about himself, but at great length, and with evident admiration, about the young poet Racine.

The King asked if he thought that Racine had strength sufficient to make him the equal of Corneille. "Sire," said the comic poet, "Racine has already surpassed Corneille by the harmonious elegance of his versification, and by the natural, true sensibility of his dialogue; his situations are never fictitious; all his words, his phrases, come from the heart. Racine alone is a true poet, for he alone is inspired."

The King, continuing, said: "I cannot witness his tragedy of 'Berenice' without shedding tears. How comes it that Madame Deshoulieres and Madame de Sevigne, who have so much mind, refuse to recognise beauties which strike a genius such as yours?"

"Sire," replied Moliere, "my opinion is nothing compared to that which your Majesty has just expressed, such is your sureness of judgment and your tact. I know by experience that those scenes of my comedies which, at a first reading, are applauded by your Majesty, always win most applause from the public afterwards."

"Is Racine in easy circumstances?" asked the King.

"He is not well off," replied Moliere, "but the tragedies which he has in his portfolio will make a rich man of him some day; of that I have not the least doubt."

"Meanwhile," said the King, "take him this draft of six thousand livres from me, nor shall this be the limit of my esteem and affection."

Five or six months after this interview, poor Moliere broke a blood-vessel in his chest, while playing with too great fervour the title part in his "Malade Imaginaire." When they brought the news to the King, he turned pale, and clasping his hands together, well-nigh burst into tears. "France has lost her greatest genius," he said before all the nobles present. "We shall never have any one like him again; our loss is irreparable!"

When they came to tell us that the Paris clergy had refused burial to "the author of 'Tartuffe,'" his Majesty graciously sent special orders to the Archbishop, and with a royal wish of that sort they were obliged to comply, or else give good reasons for not doing so.

Racine went into mourning for Moliere. The King heard this, and publicly commended such an act of good feeling and grateful sympathy.

CHAPTER XLVIII.

Madame de Montausier and the Phantom. — What She Exacts from the
Marquise. — Her Reproaches to the Duke. — Bossuet's Complacency.

Those spiteful persons who told the Queen how obliging the Duchesse de Montausier had shown herself towards me were also so extremely kind as to write an account of the whole affair to the Marquis de Montespan.

At that time he was still in Paris, and one day he went to the Duchess just as she was getting out of bed. In a loud voice he proceeded to scold her, daring to threaten her as if she were some common woman; in fact, he caught hold of her and endeavoured to strike her.

The King would not allow M. de Montausier to obtain redress from the
Marquis for such an insult as this. He granted a large pension to the Duchess, and appointed her husband preceptor to the Dauphin.

Such honours and emoluments partly recompensed the Duchess, yet they scarcely consoled her. She considered that her good name was all but lost, and what afflicted her still more was that she never recovered her health. She used to visit me, as our duties brought us together, but it was easy to see that confidence and friendship no longer existed.

One day, when passing along one of the castle corridors, which, being so gloomy, need lamplight at all hours, she perceived a tall white phantom, which glared hideously at her, and then approaching, vanished. She was utterly prostrated, and on returning to her apartments was seized with fever and shivering. The doctors perceived that her brain was affected; they ordered palliatives, but we soon saw that there was no counting upon their remedies. She was gradually sinking.

Half an hour before she died the Duchess sent for me, having given instructions that we should be left alone, and that there should be no witnesses. Her intense emaciation was pitiful, and yet her face kept something of its pleasant expression.

"It is because of you, and through you," she exclaimed in a feeble, broken voice, "that I quit this world while yet in the prime of life. God calls me; I must die.

"Kings are so horribly exacting. Everything that ministers to their passions seems feasible to them, and righteous folk must consent to do their pleasure, or suffer the penalty of being disgraced and neglected, and of seeing their long years of service lost and forgotten.

"During that unlucky journey in Brabant, you sought by redoubling your coquetry and fascinations to allure La Valliere's lover. You managed to succeed; he became fond of you. Knowing my husband's ambitious nature, he easily got him to make me favour this intrigue, and lend my apartments as a meeting-place.

"At Court nothing long remains a secret. The Queen was warned, and for a while would not believe her informants. But your husband, with brutal impetuousness, burst in upon me. He insulted me in outrageous fashion. He tried to drag me out of bed and throw me out of the window. Hearing me scream, my servants rushed in and rescued me, in a fainting state, from his clutches. And you it is who have brought upon me such scandalous insults.

"Ready to appear before my God, who has already summoned me by a spectre, I have a boon to ask of you, Madame la Marquise. I beg it of you, as I clasp these strengthless, trembling hands. Do not deny me this favour, or I will cherish implacable resentment, and implore my Master and my Judge to visit you with grievous punishment.

"Leave the King," she continued, after drying her tears. "Leave so sensual a being; the slave of his passions, the ravisher of others' good. The pomp and grandeur which surround you and intoxicate you would seem but a little thing did you but look at them as now I do, upon my bed of death.

"The Queen hates me; she is right. She despises me, and justly, too. I shall elude her hatred and disdain, which weigh thus heavily upon my heart. Perhaps she may deign to pardon me when my lawyer shall have delivered to her a document, signed by myself, containing my confession and excuses."

As she uttered these words, Madame de Montausier began to vomit blood, and I had to summon her attendants. With a last movement of the head she bade me farewell, and I heard that she called for her husband.

Next day she was dead. Her waiting-maid came to tell me that the Duchess, conscious to the last, had made her husband promise to resign his appointment as governor to the Dauphin, and withdraw to his estates, where he was to do penance. M. de Meaux, a friend of the family, read the prayers for the dying, to which the Duchess made response, and three minutes before the final death-throe, she consented to let him preach a funeral sermon in eulogy of herself and her husband.

When printed and published, this discourse was thought to be a fine piece of eloquence.

Over certain things the Bishop passed lightly, while exaggerating others. Some things, again, were entirely of his own invention; and if from the depths of her tomb the Duchess could have heard all that M. de Meaux said about her, she never would have borne me such malice, nor would her grief at leaving life and fortune have troubled her so keenly.

The King thought this funeral oration excellently well composed. Of one expression and of one whole passage, however, he disapproved, though which these were he did not do me the honour to say.